ALL MADRID

Editorial Escudo de Oro, S.A.

Plan of Madrid dating back to 1656, the work of Pedro Texeira.

THE HISTORY AND GROWTH OF THE CITY OF MADRID

Origin of the name

It used to be thought that the city had mythological origins, though these theories have since been proven to be the result more of a desire to emulate the history of other European cities than of true scientific rigour. These beliefs alternatively had Madrid founded by Ocnus, Roman king and son of a goddess who named the city Mantua, or by the Greeks. Some said the city had originally been called *Ursa* (''bear'' in Latin), due to the large number of these animals to be found in the surrounding mountains and which, along with the madrona tree, has been the symbol of the city since medieval times.

However, historical investigation came to the conclusion that the name Madrid was born with the Moorish foundation of the city. Its etymological root is ''machra'' (water) which, with the addition of ''it'' becomes ''macher-it'', meaning ''mother of abundant water''. This Moorish name refers to the wealth of waterways which existed in the sub-soil of the area, generously irrigating the city and surrounding fields. Reconquered by the Christians, the name was adapted to Castilian, becoming ''Magerit'' in medieval times and, with later transformations, ''Madrit'' and finally ''Madrid'', though pure Madrilenians generally pronounce the word ''Madrith''.

In the centre of Plaza de la Villa is the statue of Alvaro de Bazán. On the right is the Torre de la Casa de los Lujanes where, according to legend, King Francis I of France was imprisoned.

Madrid, famous castle

Archaeological discoveries on the banks of the River Manzanares prove that people have been dwelling around what is now known as Madrid for more than one hundred thousand years, since the Lower Paleolithic age, but the first recordings of Madrid's existence as a city are much more recent. Its creation is attributed to Mohamet I (852-886), emir of Cordoba, who founded Madrid as a Moorish fortress, situating it on a hill dominating the Manzanares to defend Toledo from the attacks of the troops of León and Castile.

Christian city and royal hunting grounds

With the conquest of Toledo in 1085 by Alphonse VI, Madrid fell definitively into the Christian area of influence. Its fortress was the occasional residence of the monarchs of Castile, who hunted in the surrounding woods. Fields of wheat and barley and vineyards extended around the old Moorish waterwheels and vegetable plots ("huertas"), bringing about an increase in the commercial activity of the city, which in the 14th century already possessed several permanent markets. On the outskirts were built the monasteries of San Martín and Santo Domingo. In 1202, Alphonse VIII granted special privileges ("fueros") to the city, to which more were added by successive monarchs. The Catholic Monarchs were responsible for the city's earlist urban layout. Emperor Charles V resided sporadically in Madrid and in 1534 conceded the crown on his coat of arms to the city.

Capital of the kingdom

In May 1561, Philip II named Madrid capital of the State and of the Empire. This event brought about an enormous wave of migration to the city, which tripled its population to 60,000, a rapid growth which led to a housing shortage. Attempts were made to solve this problem through the "Law of Prerogative and Lodging" and the decree of "Police and Adornment" (1591), but the Madrilenians, far from accepting the laws' restrictions, flaunted it in their "malicious" construction of new houses. During the reign of Philip IV the population rose to 100,000 and in 1625 this monarch ordered the building of the city walls which surrounded the city until 1868, occupying what is now Calle Princesa, the old boulevards leading up to Colón, Paseo del Prado, Calle Segovia and Ronda de Toledo.

The Age of Enlightenment in Madrid

The reign of the House of Bourbon saw large-scale reformation and construction work which gradually changed the image of the city. Institutions such as the Royal Academy and the Royal Library were formed and it was Charles III, the "Mayor King", who introduced the most important changes. Plans were drawn up during his reign which manifest the urban

Paseo de la Castellana and Plaza Castilla, in the centre of which is the monument to Calvo Sotelo. "La Castellana", formerly occupied by noble residences, is now characterised by high-rise buildings.

transformation of Madrid. In order to improve services and to remedy the lack of economic resources, the Royal Glass, Tapestry and Porcelain Factories were opened, and the Economic Societies of Friends of the Country (among which that of Madrid was the best known) were formed to encourage industry, agriculture and commercial development. At the end of the 18th century, in the 1797 census, Madrid had a population of nearly 170,000.

Madrid becomes a bourgeois city and its walls are demolished

The 19th century began with the French invasion, and the first third of the century marked a pause in the development of Madrid. In consequence of the first disentailments, 38 of the 68 convents disappeared and 540 properties belonging to religious orders were sold to members of the ascending bourgeoisie. New streets and squares began to be constructed at remarkable speed, as well as new houses and public buildings, in an attempt to meet the needs of a rapidly growing population, for in the mid-19th century 280,000 inhabitants dwelt within the old city walls, built in 1625. To bring relief to this state of affairs, in 1860 the Castro Plan was passed and the old walls built by Philip IV were demolished. This brought about the definition of Madrid into three zones: the old city, the new extension (bounded by the Rondas) and the outskirts. Industrialisation, too, had taken a firm hold; the traditional small factories had been joined by modern services and industries, gas, the railways, electricity, foundries, printing and the construction industry.

From 1900 to our times

At the beginning of the 20th century, Madrid had almost 580,000 inhabitants, a number which had grown to 950,000 by 1930. In 1929, to impose order on the rapid development of the city, the city council announced an international competition to find a project which, bearing in mind this inordinate rate of expansion, would draw up the most suitable plans for the extension of the city towards the north. By 1950, the population was one and a half million and ten years later it was over the two million mark. With the Stabilisation Plan of 1959, Madrid entered a period of development, with frenetic activity aimed at making the city "inhabitable" by cars: the tree-lined boulevards disappeared, flyovers and underground carparks were built and the M-30 motorway, running along course of what was the River Abroñigal, was opened. By 1970, the population of Madrid had reached three million.

Over the next decade, the character of the city changed as the bases for making it more inhabitable were laid. Districts were urbanised, a special plan protected the city's architectural heritage, circulation in the city centre was limited and public transport improved. An integral plan for a healthier city brought about the building of new parks and a new urban plan brought perspectives of a more human, rational organisation.

The application of these measures converted Madrid into one of the most pleasant and welcoming of European cities, in which architectural traces of its history stand side by side with the new streets and modern avenues.

Paseo de la Castellana, with Plaza de Emilio Castelar in the background.

Remains of the old Moorish walls in Cuesta de la Vega. In the background, the apses of the cathedral.

AN OVERALL VIEW OF THE CITY AND ITS MONUMENTS

Medieval Madrid

In the shadow of this ''famous castle'', a Moorish population grew up which inhabited a civil medina of narrow winding streets extending along the Cuesta de la Vega, Calle Mayor, crossing the hollow of Calle Segovia and stretching over the hill of Las Vistillas and the Morería district, irrigating their *huertas* from the abundant rivers and wells of the region. After the Reconquest, led by Alphonse VI, the Christian population took over the Moorish Casbah, and the two lived side by side in peace and harmony for centuries, in illustration of the characteristic quality of open, friendly city which has marked Madrid throughout its history.

Interesting are the remains of the Moorish walls, to be found in Cuesta de la Vega, the last remaining traces of those constructed in the 9th and 10th centuries by the *Moriscos* to fortify the Casbah and the tiny medina, an area little larger than the site occupied currently by the *Palacio Real* and the Plaza de Oriente.

The Mudéjar churches of San Nicolás de los Servitas and San Pedro el Viejo go back to medieval times, though all the other churches built during that period have since been lost, having been allowed by neglect to collapse through sheer old age or having been demolished during disentailment and their sites used for other purposes or in order to construct larger developments.

The House of Austria

Between Calle Bailén and the Puerta del Sol are conserved some of the most characteristic constructions dating back to this period, making up the "Madrid of the Austrias": Plaza Mayor, the *Casa de la Villa*, the Court Prison, the monasteries of Las Descalzas and of the Encarnación. This network of winding streets and tiny squares gives a glimpse of the urban layout of the city in those times.

Little remains of the palaces of this period due to the poor quality of their construction and, for the most part, their limited architectural importance. Many have been demolished or so altered that hardly anything remains of their original structure. Of the oldest, dating back to the 15th and 16th centuries, there remain a few in the Plaza de la Villa and surrounding area: the House of Los Lujanes, with its famous tower in which, according to legend, the French King Francois I was imprisoned; the old municipal newspaper library, the House of Iván de Vargas, the House of Cisneros. Dating back to the 17th century are the Palace of the Duke of Uceda, the Palace of Cañete, the House of Lope de Vega and that of the Seven Chimneys ("La Casa de las Siete Chimeneas").

Paintings by Rizzi and Carreño adorn the ceiling and walls of the Church of San Antonio de los Alemanes.

La Casa de las Siete Chimeneas (Seven Chimneys).

Façade of the Palacio de Vistahermosa, which now houses the Thyssen Bornemisza Museum.

In the 17th century, with the definitive establishment of the court in Madrid, and stimulated by the competitive patronage of monarchs, noblemen, religious orders and congregations, a proliferation of churches and convents were built. However, only in certain rare cases did the restrictions imposed by the city's urban layout allow the construction of large buildings, there being hardly space for the pretentious fronts of the heyday of the Baroque period to be appreciated. This obstacle led architects to seek a solution in height, through the construction of spectacular towers and domes, rather than in façades, and these became the dominant features of the various churches built. It is for this reason that in 17th- and 18th-century engravings of the city its

outline is characterised by stylised capitals, due to the large number of churches and convents featuring this element of architectural design. A multitude of such examples remain: the Cathedral of San Isidro and the churches and convents of Las Carboneras del Corpus, El Carmen Calzado, Las Trinitarias Descalzas, Las Calatravas, San Ginés, Las Agustinas Recoletas de Santa Isabel, Las Bernardas de Sacramento, La Venerable Orden Tercera, San Antonio de los Alemanes, Las Benedictinas de San Plácido, Las Mercedarias Descalzas, Las Comendadoras de Santiago, San Sebastián and the Chapel of San Isidro.

The Bourbons and the Enlightenment

The Age of Enlightenment caused the monarchs of

Spain to see the need for modernisation. Madrid, as the capital, became a privileged beneficiary of this concern and its accesses, outskirts, infrastructure and public services made their greatest advances in terms of quality during this period. Many buildings with institutional and scientific purposes were constructed: the Post Office, the Customs Building, the Royal Academies, the House of the Ministers, the Five Principal Guilds, the Barracks of the Count-Duke, the Hospice, the Salon of the Prado, the General Hospital of San Carlos and the Puerta de Alcalá.

In the early 18th century, in imitation of the court, the aristocracy began to build their palaces with emphasis on exterior appearance as a sign of social status. Dating back to the first half of this century, in pure Baroque style, though since much altered, are the palaces of Ugena, of Miraflores and of Perales, all works by Pedro de Ribera. The most outstanding palaces were built during the second half of the 18th century when, with Neo-Classical tastes, the nobility constructed beautiful residences surrounded by walls and gardens which adorned the streets and districts where they stood. Examples of this period are the palaces of Liria, Buenavista and Vistahermosa. The foremost architects of the day, Ventura Rodríguez, Sabatini, Juan de Villanueva and Antonio López Aguado all made a contribution to these ambitious works, of which the most outstanding is, of course, the *Palacio Nuevo,* constructed as the residence of the royal family.

In contrast to the previous century, in the 18th century the construction of religious buildings diminished.

Main front of the Palacio de Liria, constructed in the second half of the 18th century.

and greater care was taken over the quality of the new additions which, over the course of this period, took different artistic forms: representing the Baroque are the churches of San Cayetano, Montserrat, San José, San Miguel and the Salesas Reales; works in the transitional style to Neo-Classical include those of San Marcos, Santiago and San Francisco el Grande; and, finally, in pure Neo-Classical style, the Oratory of the Caballero de Gracia.

Madrid during the reign of Isabel II

In the 19th century, it was the bourgeoisie who built the finest palaces and promoted urban reform. Architectural forms were eclectic and individual taste was catered to in an age where it was possible to commission a "made to measure" palace. In the new districts of Salamanca and Argüelles (developments promoted by the marquises of Salamanca and Pozas) and in the districts of Las Salesas, Los Jerónimos and Recoletas, the new bourgeoisie of Madrid founded their residences. The counterpoint to this was the rise of the working class districts of Vallehermosa, Tetuán de las Victorias and the areas east of Narvaéz and El Retiro, on the outskirts of the city. In the centre, the poor huddled in the typical *corralas*, dwellings organised around a central patio or yard, the settings of the plays of Ramón de la Cruz and other Madrilenian writers.

The 19th century saw a spectacular boom in the construction of public buildings. During this time, the Congress, the Senate, the Stock Exchange, the National Library and the Bank of Spain were all completed, whilst the sciences were fostered through the creation of university faculties and colleges and institutions such as the Madrid Atheneum. Urban reform and development took place at the Puerta del Sol and Plaza de Oriente and public works included the installation of gas lighting and the building of the Isabel II Canal and the railways.

The Almudena Cathedral and the Church of Santa Cruz were the only religious buildings of magnitude completed in the 19th century, both commissioned by and in the eclectic style of the Marquis of Cubas.

Front of the Ateneo.

20th-century Madrid

Various great works were undertaken: the extension of Paseo de la Castellana, the creation of the *Ciudad Lineal* of Arturo Soria, whilst great luxury hotels such as the Ritz and the Palace were built, the Metro was inaugurated, the outskirts of the city and accesses and railway connections were developed, the Gran Via was completed, the University City was constructed, the new ministerial buildings came into being, the waters of the Manzanares were brought under control and the *Casa de Campo* was opened. During the 1950s, skyscrapers were built around Plaza de España, new middle-class districts sprang up on the outskirts of the city and Madrid absorbed the surrounding villages to become the great metropolitan area it is today.

Over the past few decades, Madrid has become a modern city, transforming areas such as the Castellana, Plaza de Colón and Plaza de Castilla, whilst new districts have been constructed in which some of the finest examples of contemporary architecture are to be found, such as the AZCA block of buildings.

On arriving in the city, the first impression the visitor receives is one of everybody being in a hurry. However, one must not be taken in by this sensation, for one of the most marvellous experiences the city offers is the chance to stroll around its streets, slowly discovering its monuments and enjoying the intense life of the capital. This guide describes some ideal spots for this type of leisurely activity.

The AZCA complex, flagship of avant-garde architecture in Madrid.

Plaza de Oriente with the monument to Philip IV in the centre, and the main front of the Palacio Real.

PALACES

Palacio Real (Calle de Bailén)

The old *Alcázar*, fortress, a cold and inhospitable 9th-century Moorish construction, extended by the Bourbons, was completely burnt down on Christmas Eve 1734 in one of the fastest and most terrible fires recorded. The flames devoured a marvellous collection of paintings and *objets d'art*, but also gave the new Bourbon dynasty the opportunity to fashion a building more appropriate as the setting for the official activities of the country and as the royal residence, following the example set by the principal courts of Europe. Philip V summoned Filippo Juvara from Italy and proposed that he build a huge building comparable to the Palace of Versailles in the style of Bernini's project for the Louvre, though, due to its size, located outside the city centre. Shortly after completing the plans, Juvara died and the king commissioned his pupil Giovanni Battista Sachetti to carry out the work, imposing the condition that he must use the site of the old *Alcázar*.

Sachetti began construction with the intention that what the palace lost in extension should be gained in height, and ensured that the new building should be fire-proof by using only stone as his materials. The first stone was laid in 1738 and it is said that the foundations reached the same depth as the River Manzanares, which runs at the foot of the slopes on which the Palace stands. Building, in which the ar-

The throne room in the Palacio Real.

chitects Sabatini and Ventura Rodríguez also intervened, was completed in 1764, and the first monarch to make his residence here was Charles III. The overall design is in the style of Baroque Classicism, whilst there is a mixture of French and Italian influences in the elements used its in construction and decoration. This splendid building forms a quadrilateral made up of four almost identical fronts and the series of pillars and embedded columns and the combination of granite and white stone are perhaps the most outstanding features of its composition. The solid basement of bossed ashlar which makes up the ground floor gives emphasis to the classical elegance of the main floor, which features embedded supports and finely-designed windows between the columns. The whole is crowned by a balustrade.

The Palace is now used for state occasions, whilst part houses a museum of obligatory visit, for it offers the chance to appreciate one of the best-furnished palaces of Europe. In fact, the original furniture has been conserved, and outstanding amongst its dependencies being the rooms decorated by Gasparini, formerly the private chambers of Charles III, the throne room and the state dining room. Innumerable works of art adorn the Palace: there are ceilings decorated by Corrado Giaquinto, Tiepolo and Mengs, and works by Goya, Watteau, Van der Weyden, Bosch, Velázquez and Caravaggio. The demands of protocol and the social life of the

Gala dining room in the Palacio Real.

monarchs caused a wealth of sumptuous objects to be accumulated here, now part of the Palace collections, and which were enriched over various reigns. These collections have incalculable artistic, historic and documentary value, containing some of the most important pieces of their type; tapestries, porcelain, gold and silver work, royal mantles, religious robes, clocks, sculptures, bronzes, chandeliers, furniture, carpets, etc.

Several monographic museums, each with extraordinary collections, are housed within the building: the Music Museum, with a Stradivarius quintet; the Royal Library, with more than 300,000 volumes and incunabulae; the Royal Pharmacy, with a 17th-century alchemy laboratory; the Royal Armoury, a collection founded by Philip II to gather together and conserve his and his father's weapons, considered one of the finest in the world of its type; and the Carriage Museum, a collection of vehicles used by the monarchs from the 16th to the 20th centuries, servants' uniforms, saddles and horse-riding equipment. The site on which the *Palacio Real* stands is one of the most beautiful areas of the city and among the most splendid both architecturally and in terms of town planning as, when construction began, the plans also included consideration of the surrounding area. In this way, a noble setting was provided for the Palace. The cathedral, the gardens, Calle Bailén with the viaduct crossing Calle Segovia, the slopes of the Cuesta de San Vicente leading to the *Casa del*

Campo, the stables and the barracks, were all designed at the same time as the *Palacio Real,* though they were constructed at later dates during the 19th and even the 20th centuries.

Palacio de la Liria (Calle de la Princesa, 20)
Surrounded by lovely gardens which obscure the view from beyond the walls of its splendid Neo-Classical front, this is, without doubt, the most magnificent example of a noble residence to be found in Madrid. It was begun in 1773 according to the project by Sabatini and Ventura Rodríguez, commissioned by Jacobo Stuart Fitzjames, third duke of Berwick and Liria, married to a sister of the Duke of Alba. The residence, which belongs now to the House of Alba, contains a fine art collection.

Palace of the Marquis of Salamanca
(Paseo de Recoletos, 10)
Now the seat of the Banco Hipotecario, this is one of the most magnificent palaces constructed by the powerful new bourgeoisie of the 19th century. The Marquis of Salamanca, banker and patron of public works during the reign of Isabel II, commissioned Narciso Pascual y Colomer with the construction of this Italian Neo-Renaissance-style building.

Palace of the Marquis of Salamanca, now seat of the Banco Hipotecario.

Convent of the Descalzas Reales: front and main steps.

CHURCHES AND CONVENTS

Monastery of the Descalzas Reales
(Plaza de las Descalzas Reales, 3)
Founded by Princess Joan of Austria, daughter of Emperor Charles V, this monastery occupies a palace which formerly belonged to Alonso Gutiérrez, the emperial treasurer. When the *Alcázar* became the official residence of Philip II, the palace was placed at the disposal of his mother, the Empress Isabel, and it was here that the founder of the monastery was born in the summer of 1535, ''in the cool rooms overlooking the large *huerta*''. The work of transforming the palace into a convent were directed by Antonio Sillero and Juan Bautista de Toledo (author of the original designs for El Escorial) from 1556 to 1564, and work was continued in the 17th century by Juan Gómez de Mora. The front of the church is an austere, beautiful composition in the style of the Escorial, over which is emblazoned the coat of arms of its founder.

For centuries, the wives and daughters of royalty and the aristocracy worshipped or were guests here, and this is the reason behind the extraordinary accumulation of works of art to be found in the convent. To judge by the splendid collections of religious art, portraits and tapestries housed in the museum (opened to the public, previously not allowed admittance to the convent, in 1960) an important part of the withdrawn life of these women was aesthetic contemplation. Amongst the many 15th- to 17th-century works contained here, outstanding are the decoration of the staircase, with splendid effects of perspective, attributed to Claudio Coello, paintings by Pieter Bruegel I, Pantoja de la Cruz, Zurbarán, Titian and Sánchez Coello, as well as a room adorned by tapestries based on cartoons by Rubens. Also exhibited are the work of such religious painters as Pedro de Mena and Gregorio Hernández and a magnificent collection of liturgical ornaments. This museum has been declared of World Interest.

Convent of the Encarnación
(Plaza de la Encarnación, 1)

Founded by Queen Margaret of Austria, spouse of Philip III, it took five years to complete the construction of the convent, which was blessed in 1616 in solemn ceremony. Its architect was the young Juan Gómez de Mora, who followed the basic ideas of his uncle and master, Francisco de Mora, author of San José in Avila. The front, harmoniously constructed in beautiful ashlar and brick, became the model for the churches of the Carmelites for several decades,

Convent of the Encarnación: front and the chapel which contains the reliquary with the blood of Saint Pantaleon.

Church of San Isidro, which contains the body of Saint Isidoro, patron saint of the city.

with slight variations. The church suffered a fire in the mid-18th century and Ventura Rodríguez, commissioned to restore the interior, employed a wealth of jasper, marble and bronze in accordance with the tastes of Bourbon times.

The church is popular in Madrid as it contains a reliquary containing the blood of Saint Pantaleón, which liquifies every 27 July. Besides this, the museum contains many more reliquaries and an excellent collection of paintings, sculptures and religious art, as well as a remarkable collection of liturgical objects and other interesting items accumulated through the gifts of the noblewomen who worshipped at the convent or through the donations of its illustrious guests.

Church of San Isidro (Calle de Toledo, 37 and 39)

Two Jesuit architects, Francisco Bautista and Pedro Sánchez, were the authors of the project for this church, formerly the chapel of the Imperial College. The main front, its enormous columns set according to the colossal order of Michelangelo, cannot be appreciated from the front due to the narrowness of the street, but gain in perspective and effect when viewed from one side. In a niche in the centre is a statue of Saint Isidro. The railings are crowned by the two-headed eagle, symbol of the Austrian dynasty, founders of the College. In the interior, deposited in two urns by the high altar are the remains of the patron saint of Madrid, Saint Isidro, and of his wife, Saint Mary of the Head. Though the cathedral was commenced in 1622, the interior decoration by Ventura Rodríguez dates back to the mid-18th century.

Church of the Salesas Reales, the only surviving element from the formerly extensive convent.

Convent of the Salesas Reales
(Calle de Bárbara de Braganza)

The construction of this convent was commissioned by Bárbara of Braganza, wife of Ferdinand VI, as a college for the daughters of the nobility. It was built between 1750 and 1758 by Francisco Carlier in monumental Baroque style and at enormous expense by the standards of the day, beside a royal residence which the queen was never to inhabit. Inside the church are the remains of both monarchs, buried there at their express wish, breaking the custom of burying members of the royal family at the Monastery of El Escorial. The beautiful railings and the stairway leading up to the church were built at the beginning of the 20th century.

Basilica of San Francisco el Grande
(Plaza de San Francisco)

Founded in the 13th century, when Saint Francis of Assissi personally chose this as the site for a modest monastery, it became a focal point towards which the city expanded, and when the monastery was demolished in the 18th century the church contained twenty-five chapels and the tombs of some forty illustrious figures. The new church was built in the Neo-Classical style popular at the time, according to the plans of Fray Francisco Cabezas, whose conception was of a circular building covered by an imposing dome 33 metres in diameter. However, it was completed in 1776 by Sabatini, who solved the problems caused by the enormous size of the dome. Its outstanding feature is the huge front organised in two high storeys, supporting the dome. The interior contains ''San Bernadino'', one of Goya's earliest works.

San Francisco el Grande: main front.

Church of San Jerónimo el Real, restored several times since its construction in the 15th century.

San Jerónimo el Real (Calle de Moreto, 4)

This is a peculiar building due to the successive reforms to which it was submitted and to its historical importance to the city and the court. In 1462, Henry IV of Castile founded a Hieronymite monastery on the old route to El Pardo. In 1501 the Catholic Monarchs, due to the deterioration which this monastery had suffered, decided to rebuild it on the site it presently occupies. Work was completed on this Gothic construction in 1505, and in 1510 the first court of Ferdinand the Catholic was assembled here. Since that time, the church has been the traditional scene of the investiture of the princes of Asturias, the proclamation of kings and queens, royal weddings and other solemn occasions. It was also a place of retreat for royalty, for since the time of Charles I there has been an "Old Room" here, where monarchs resided in times of mourning and during Lent. Over the centuries, the building was extended until it became the original nucleus of the great Palace of El Buen Retiro, built by the Count-Duke of Olivares for Philip IV. The 19th century was a period of great suffering for the Church and Sant Jerónimo's was partially destroyed. Later, at the desire of Isabel II, it was restored by Narciso Pascual i Colomer in a style which took its inspiration from Late-Gothic Castilian architecture.

Cathedral of the Almudena.

Shrine of San Antonio de la Florida.

Cathedral of the Almudena (Cuesta de la Vega)
Commissioned in 1880, though only the Neo-Romanesque crypt was finished at that time, by the Marquis of Cubas, and constructed in his characteristic eclectic style, the cathedral is a monumental work of medieval inspiration, executed in classical Gothic style. Its verticality and medieval quality is in stark contrast with the horizontal lines and classical style of the adjacent *Palacio Real,* of which it is a continuation according to the original 18th-century plans. The main front, with two identical, symmetrical towers, was finally completed in 1960, with huge differences to the original plans. The church is dedicated to the Virgin of La Almudena, patron saint of the city, worshipped since earliest times. According to legend, during the Moorish occupation the Christian inhabitants hid the statue of the Virgin in a fold of the wall (''almudaina'' in Arabic) or in a grain store (''almudit'') nearby, and it was miraculously discovered when Alphonse VI reconquered Madrid on 9 November 1085. Since then, the statue of the Virgin Mary has received the name of Almudena, a popular girl's name in Madrid.

Shrines
Three shrines in Madrid deserve special mention. That of the *Virgen del Puerto*, in the street of the same name, was built in 1718 by Pedro de Ribera, commissioned by the Marquis of Vadillo, mayor of the city. In pure Baroque style, the shrine was built so that the washerwomen who worked on the banks of the Manzanares could attend mass. San Antonio de la Florida (Glorieta de San Antonio de la Florida) was built during the reign of Charles IV by Felipe Fontana in Neo-Classical style, and contains frescoes by Goya, painted in 1798 using advanced techniques for the time. The Shrine of San Isidro is of little artistic interest, but acquires importance due to the *romería* which takes place here on that saint's day and whose rich atmosphere is reflected in various works by Goya.

The Parliament building, opposite Plaza de las Cortes.

Main front of the Senate building.

PUBLIC BUILDINGS

Congress (Plaza de las Cortes)
This is perhaps, after the *Palacio Real,* the most finely executed and important architectural work in Madrid. It was built on the site of the old Church of the Espíritu Santo, where parliament had met since 1834. The Royal Academy of San Fernando chose the project by Narciso Pascual y Colomer, whose design was inspired by the Italian palaces of the 15th century, with the addition of a Corinthian portico with classical pediment. The first stone was laid by Isabel II in 1843 and the building was completed in 1850. The two lions flanking the entrance were cast in 1860 in metal from cannons captured during the war in Africa.

Senate (Plaza de la Marina Española)
This occupies the reformed former Calced Augustines monastery, rebuilt in the early 19th century and containing since 1814 the Sessions Chamber of the General Courts of the Kingdom, where six years later Ferdinand VII swore loyalty to the constitution. The interior is decorated with a fine collection of historical paintings, much appreciated in the second half of the 19th century. The monument at the entrance is to Cánovas del Castillo, a 19th-century politician.

The National Library is one of the most solemn of the Elizabethan buildings in Madrid.

National Library (Paseo de Recoletos, 18)

This was built to replace the Royal Library, created in 1712 by Philip V. The present building was begun by Francisco Jareño in 1892 in the classicist style popular at the time and now contains more than five million books, manuscripts, incunabulae, pamphlets, prints, engravings and magazines. Its most important treasures include the codex of "Mío Cid" and a collection of editions of "Don Quijote"; more than 3,000 volumes including translations into over thirty languages.

The Stock Exchange (Plaza de la Lealtad)

Founded in 1813 by royal decree of Ferdinand VII, though the original idea corresponds to Joseph I. The Stock Exchange had at least half a dozen homes before finally being installed in this building, constructed in 1884 by the architect Repullés y Vargas in the Official style of the period.

Observatory (Park of El Retiro)

Constructed at the initiative of Jorge Juan, who suggested to King Charles III the creation of an Astronomy Lecture Hall to complement the monarch's idea of promoting the sciences, though work was not finally commenced until 1790, during the reign of Charles IV. The building, designed by Villanueva, is one of the purest exponents of Neo-Classicism to be found in Madrid, and is formed by a dome flanked by four quadrangular bodies in the form of a cross. Impressive are the elegance of the portico with its Corinthian columns and the grace of the upper pavilion.

Royal Customs House (Calle de Alcalá, 11)

Designed by Sabatini in 1769, commissioned by Charles III. This Neo-Classical building has an austere, unadorned front in which the outstanding feature is

The Stock Exchange, whose architectural style was inspired by its counterpart in Vienna.

Entrance to the Conde Duque Barracks, garrison of Philip V's royal guard, now an important cultural centre.

the bossed ground floor, which gives a rounded effect to this building, crowned by an enormous cornice. The design is heavily influenced by the Roman-style palaces of the time. The Customs House is currently occupied by the Ministry of the Exchequer.

Tobacco Factory (Calle de Embajadores, 55)
One of the few remaining examples of 18th-century industrial architecture. Constructed in 1790 for the manufacture of liquors, whiskeys, cards and stamped paper, it was during the reign of Joseph Bonaparte that it began to be used for the manufacture of cigars and snuff.

Barracks of the Count-Duke
(Calle del Conde Duque, 9)
Built in 1720 by Pedro de Ribera, this is an enormous rectangular building structured around three courtyards of which the central square is the largest. The basic material used was brick, simply decorated, which gives emphasis to the large stone entrance, profusely adorned with sculptures featuring flags, coats of arms and military trophies.

El Hospicio (calle de Fuencarral, 78)
The building presently houses the City Museum and Library, and is an architectural masterpiece by Pedro de Ribera. Work began in 1722, but the *Hospicio General de Pobres del Ave María* was not completed until 1799. This Baroque building has an splendid portal, criticised by Neo-Classicists for over a century due to the exhuberance of the decorative elements; mouldings, coats of arms, drapery, urns, flowers, etc. A niche over the door contains a statue of Saint Ferdinand by Juan Ron. Leafy gardens at the back contain the Fountain of Fame, designed by Pedro de Ribera in his characteristically flamboyant style.

Museum and Municipal Library, featuring a Baroque front.

The Puerta de Alcalá, one of the most representative monuments in Madrid.

The Puerta de Alcalá, formerly the entranceway to the walled city. ▷

Court Prison (Plaza de la Provincia)
Now the Ministry of Foreign Affairs, this building was constructed in the 17th century by Cristóbal de Aguilera after plans by Gómez de Villarreal. The main front, an example of Madrilenian Baroque, is framed by two spired towers, the brick used in them contrasting with the stone of the imposts, chains, balcony openings and central doorway, central decorative elements. Built to replace the old prison, in which Lope de Vega is said to have been held, due to its poor security, its opening ended the tradition of holding prisoners in the houses of ordinary citizens.

OUTSTANDING MONUMENTS

Alcalá Gate (Plaza de la Independencia)
This is undoubtedly the most famous and representative monument in the city. Commissioned as a triumphal arch by King Charles III in his desire to endow the city with worthy entrances, the work was entrusted to Francisco Sabatini. The design is in the purest Neo-Classical style, broken only by the sculptural decorations by Francisco Gutiérrez and Roberto Michel. Built in granite and white stone from Colmenar, it has five spans, those at either end

The Puerta de Toledo, another of the entrances to the walled city in ancient times. Building began during the short reign of Joseph Bonaparte and was completed under Ferdinand VII, to whom it is dedicated.

FERNANDO VII R. H. OPTATISSIMO. REDVO.
TYRANNIDE GALLORVM EXCVSSA.
ORDO MATRITENSVM
FIDEI· VICTORIAE· LAETITIAE· MONVMENTVM. D.
ANN. M DCCC. XX. VII.

formed by flat arches, the three central spaces formed by semicircular arches. Though all are of the same height, the central arch appears higher due its upper attic storey. The monument is decorated with Ionic pilasters and columns.

Toledo Gate (Plaza de Toledo)

This area was developed during the reign of King Charles III, but the gate was begun under Joseph I and was completed in the time of Ferdinand VII. This is a Neo-Classic work by Antonio López Aguado (1827) and is crowned by allegories of Spain protecting the Arts.

Segovia Bridge (at the end of Calle de Segovia)

This bridge and the Toledo Bridge are perhaps the oddest monuments in Madrid, for their rich architecture contrasts with the small size of the River Manzanares. The bridge was commissioned by Philip II who, having established Madrid as the capital of Spain, wished to endow the city with fine monuments. In 1532, the royal architect, Juan de Herrera, designed a solid bridge of austere line, its only decoration being the Renaissance rhythm of its arches and the typical Herreran balls on the parapets.

The Segovia Bridge with, left, the Shrine of the Virgen del Puerto.

The Puente de Toledo, the Aqueduct and a partial view of Puerta de Atocha station.

Toledo Bridge
(between Pirámides and Marqués de Vadillo)
Constructed during the reign of Philip V, though its true impulsor was the Marquis of Vadillo, mayor of the city from 1715 to 1729, who realised the need to replace the old wooden bridge crossing the river at this busy point to facilitate the entrance of supplies to the city from La Mancha. Pedro de Ribera was commissioned with the construction of the bridge in his characteristic Baroque style. The granite monument is formed by five equal arches with, on either side of the central arch, two fine niches containing statues of Saint Isidro and Saint Mary of the Head, by Juan Ron.

The Viaduct (Calle de Bailén)
This joins the Palace area with that of Las Vistillas. Though part of the original plans for the Palacio Real, it was not finally constructed until the late-19th century, and was made of iron. The present viaduct, opened in 1942, is the work of the architect Francisco Javier Ferrero and the engineers José Juan Aracil and Luis Aldaz, who employed reinforced concrete.

Puerta de Atocha station
(Glorieta del Emperador Carlos V)
tion, on the Madrid-Aranjuez line, popularly known as the "strawberry train". This was destroyed by fire and the new station was built in 1892 by Alberto de Palacio. This consists of two brick pavilions between which is the great glass and iron roof. There is now a tropical garden under this roof, installed after the massive reforms carried out to house the highspeed railway line (AVE).

The well-known Puerta del Sol, with its elliptical groundpland. To the left is the former post office building, now seat of the President of the Autonomous Community of Madrid.

Kilometre 0 and the statue of Mariblanca, in the Puerta del Sol.

SQUARES

Puerta del Sol

This has always been one of the most popular areas of Madrid, and so has been the scene of important events in the history of the city and of Spain: the uprising of 2 May 1808, depicted in Goya's painting of the same name; the proclamation of the Second Republic in 1931; the first gas lighting, switched on in 1830; and the inauguration of the first line of the Metro, Sol-Quatro Caminos, in 1919. It also contains Kilometre 0 of the roads of Spain.

Originally, in the 15th century, this area was part of the outskirts of the city, surrounded by a wall with a gate "facing the sun", hence its name. From 1560 onwards, various buildings, together with the bookshops, cheap eating houses and jewellers' shops established there, brought about a rivalry with the Plaza Mayor over which was the city centre. Later, the popular Mariblanca Fountain was added, of which a copy remains on a column at one of the corners of the square.

During the reign of Isabel II, plans drawn up by Lucio del Valle, Juan Rivera and José Morer gave it the definitive elliptical shape it has now. Of the original buildings, only the post office building, now seat of the Autonomous Government of Madrid, was conserved. This dates back to 1761 and is the work of Jaime Marquet, its famous clock marking the arrival of each New Year. Recently, its lamps, fountains, benches, canopies and kiosks were restored, the fronts repainted and traffic diverted. This renovation caused great controversy and due to public demand the modern lamps were replaced by the old ones dating back to the times of Ferdinand.

The bear and the madrona tree, emblematic symbols of the city of Madrid, in the Puerta del Sol. ⟩

Plaza Mayor

This was constructed by Juan Gómez de Mora, commissioned by Philip II, who desired to build a great square which would give prestige to his kingdom. The site chosen was the former Plaza del Arrabal, the setting of an important market since the 16th century. Work began in 1617 and was completed two years later. The rational project, in Madrilenian Baroque style characteristic of the period of the Austrias, was an innovation in town planning in the city. The plans left standing the *Casa de la Panadería,* on whose ground floor was a bakery built by Diego Sillero in 1590 and, opposite, the *Casa de la Carnicería.* The arcades contain a large number of shops and craftsmen's workshops.

The square contains 136 houses, with 437 balconies from which 50,000 people were able to witness the many events held here, tourneys, bull fights, the proclamations of monarchs, royal weddings, autos-da-fé, executions and local festivities. The beatification and canonisation of Saint Isidro and other popular saints such as Santa Teresa de Jesús also took place here. The character of this square has remained unaltered over the years, and is still a meeting-place and the site of evening strolls of many Madrilenians. In the centre is a statue of Philip III, impulsor of the construction of this fine square and first king of the Austria dynasty to be born in Madrid, by Pietro Tacca.

Overall view of Plaza Mayor.

Casa de la Panaderia and the monument to Philip III, in Plaza Mayor. ▷

Plaza de la Villa

An important square in the history of the city, for Madrid has been governed from here since time immemorial. The locals used to meet in the Church of San Salvador and were granted the right to organise their own local government in the 14th century by Alphonse XI. In this way, the Madrid City Council came into being and it was decided to build a City Hall on the site of the now demolished church. Finally, however, a typical Madrilenian Baroque building was commenced in 1640 on a nearby site. Since its completion, this has been the City Hall, its architecture untouched except for the balcony overlooking the Calle Mayor, constructed by Juan de Villanueva for the queen and her attendants to watch the procession of Corpus Christi.

The square has an irregular shape and contains various interesting buildings dating back to the 15th and 16th centuries, some of the oldest in the city. However, the most attractive aspect of the square and surrounding streets is the peacefulness which instils them, making this visit to the Madrid of the Austrias a veritable pleasure. In the centre of the square is a statue of Don Alvaro de Bazán by Mariano Benlliure (1888).

Madrid City Council Building, in Plaza de la Villa.

Plaza de Oriente, with the Palacio Real in the background.

Plaza de Oriente

Its name is due to the fact that the square adjoins the eastern front of the *Palacio Real,* and its construction to Joseph Bonaparte's wish to create a space from where the beauty of this monumental palace could be contemplated. Development of the square was completed in the time of Isabel II according to plans drawn up by Agustín Argüelles and Martín de los Heros.

The central statue of Philip IV was laid in 1843 and is a beautiful 17th-century sculpture, in whose completion various artists worked: Pietro Tacca sculpted the bronze after the model by Martínez Montañés; the head is a copy of that of the equestrian portrait by Velázquez and Galileo Galilei calculated the centre of gravity to ensure the equilibrium of the statue. Subsequently, the statues of other monarchs,

originally intended for the balustrade of the *Palacio Real,* were placed in the gardens.

The buildings surrounding the square date back to the 19th century. One of the most interesting of these is the *Teatro Real.* In remote times, this was the site of the fountains and washing place of the district, also known as the Caños del Peral. In 1704, a group of travelling actors made their home here, giving origin to the theatre which stood here until the early-19th century. In 1818 this was pulled down due to its ruinous state and plans were drawn up by Antonio López Aguado for the Royal Theatre. Work on this was held up repeatedly until its eventual completion in 1850 by express order of Isabel II, and the theatre was inaugurated on 19 November of that year with a performance of Donizetti's ''La Favorita''.

Front of the Teatro Real and the monument to Philip IV, in Plaza de Oriente.

The luxuriant gardens in El Campo del Moro with, in the foreground, the fountain known as the Fuente de los Tritones.

The Cibeles Fountain, a marble sculpture which has become a symbol of Madrid.

Plaza de Cibeles

This is one of the most famous and popular of the squares of Madrid. In its centre is the statue of the Goddess Cybele, with a fountain commissioned by Charles III to complete one of the sides of the Salon of the Prado. The drawing was by Ventura Rodríguez and the sculptures of the lions and the statue are by Roberto Michel and Francisco Gutiérrez. Its views of the surrounding avenues and streets and the fine buildings surrounding the square make this one of the most beautiful sights in the city.

The Banco de España was created by Echegaray in 1874 as the sole issuing bank, and the building was completed from 1884 to 1891 by Eduardo Adaro and Severiano Sainz in a style inspired by Italian and French architecture. Many works of art, including paintings by Goya, are housed here.

The *Palacio de Comunicaciones* was constructed by

Plaza de la Cibeles, a popular spot.

the architects Palacios and Otamendi, and its interior design was highly innovative for its time. The huge front was completed in Monumental style.

The *Palacio de Linares* is one of the finest examples of 19th-century palace architecture, with a beautiful Neo-Baroque façade. Its designer was Carlos Colubi, commissioned by a businessman accorded the title of Marquis of Linares.

The *Palacio de Buenavista*, now occupied by Army Headquarters, was constructed at the end of the 18th century by Juan Pedro Arnal as the residence of Cayetano de Alba, the duchess immortalised by Goya, who died leaving his portrait of her unfinished. Later the building belonged to Manuel Godoy, prime minister to Charles III and Prince of Peace.

Plaza de España.

Plaza de España

This huge esplanade serves both as meeting-point and important traffic nexus. The plane trees on the south side form a pleasant, leafy border to the gardens in the centre, in which is the monument to Cervantes, designed in 1915 by Teodoro Anasagasti and Mateo Inurria, whose intention was to celebrate in it the essence of the Hispanic character. The square features two skyscrapers built in the 1950s to crown the Gran Vía, by the brothers Otamendi.

Detail of the monument to Cervantes, in Plaza de España.

The monument to Cervantes is situated in the centre of Plaza de España. On the left is the Torre de Madrid and in the background the Edificio España.

Plaza de Colón

The Gardens of the Discovery occupy the centre of the square, presided over, on the east side, by huge allegorical sculptures by Turcios, representing the heroic voyage of Columbus. In one corner of the square is the Neo-Gothic monument to that explorer, designed by Arturo Mélida in 1885.

Under the square is the Centro Cultural de la Villa de Madrid, hidden behind a beautiful and noisy curtain of water. The centre contains a concert hall, exhibition rooms and a theatre for social and cultural events. Lastly, in 1976 the ''Torres de Colón'' were built, huge towers in the then revolutionary style of ''hanging'' architecture, by Antonio Lamela.

Plaza de Colón and the Gardens of the Discovery.

Various views of Plaza de Colón: the Torres de Colón and the underground entrance to the Centro Cultural de la Villa; the monument to Columbus; and sculptures in the Gardens of the Discovery.

Fuente de Neptuno, in Paseo del Prado.

WALKS AND SITES OF INTEREST

Paseo del Prado

Always a popular area for walks, this zone was formerly part of the outskirts of the city, a pleasant spot with trees and *huertas* watered by the stream which ran from north to south. So it was throughout the 17th century, but in the 18th it was converted into an exponent of the illuminated ideas of the time by Charles III and his minister, the Count of Aranda. This involved the creation of a scientific and cultural area harmonising aspects of utility, beauty and diversion. Plans for this transformation were drawn up by José Hermosilla, who levelled land, canalised and covered the stream and altered the layout of the plantations to maintain the shadows of their trees whilst leaving a wide avenue, for which Ventura Rodríguez designed the great monumental fountains we can now admire: the Cuatro Fuentes of the Plaza Murillo, on either side of the avenue, of marble from Redueña; the Fountain of Neptune, sculpted in marble from Montesclaros by Juan Pascual de Mena, who represented the god on a chariot in the form of a snail, pulled by sea horses; the Fountain of Apollo, with a high pedestal surrounded by the four seasons, the work of the sculptors Giraldo Bergaz and Manuel Alvarez; and lastly, at the end of the avenue and in the square bearing her name, the fountain of the goddess Cybele.

Though never finally built, a columned arcade was planned on on side of the avenue, in which were to be situated cafés and chocolate shops. The other side was devoted to research buildings, with the construction of the Botanical Gardens and the Natural History Museum, now the Museum of the Prado, both designed by Juan de Villanueva in the Neo-

Classical style which dominates the entire Paseo del Prado.

Even today, the avenue retains its original character as a promenade, and is always full of visitors to the museums. This is a most pleasant spot due to the width of the avenue and the gardens, fountains and magnificent buildings lining it. Among these buildings are the Stock Exchange and the Monument to the Unknown Soldier, 19th-century constructions situated in the Plaza de la Lealtad.

Plaza Cánovas del Castillo - Fountain of Neptune.

Paseo de Recoletos.

Paseo de Recoletos and Paseo de la Castellana

These avenues were constructed in the 19th century as a consequence of the expansion of the city to the north. Designed to be aristocratic, peaceful areas, they were chosen by the bourgeoisie as the site of their palaces, now mostly lost or transformed from residences into the seats of financial or official institutions. Even so, despite the heavy traffic circulating around its streets, it is still possible to take a walk along the gardens in the centre of the avenues, in which there are lively pavement bars, especially attractive on summer evenings.

Paseo de la Castellana has become the favoured site for the headquarters of banks and enterprises, and many buildings representative of the latest architectural tendencies have been constructed here. The central boulevard is a splendid setting for walks in the shadow of its trees to the Open Air Sculpture Museum, located under the pedestrian bridge joining Paseo del Cisne with Calle Juan Bravo. The museum houses a collection of Spanish vanguardist sculptural works by Julio González, Manuel Rivera, Andrés Alfaro, Eusebio Sempere, Eduardo Chillida and Joan Miró, amongst others.

In Plaza San Juan de la Cruz, there is the Nuevos Ministerios building, constructed on the site of the former Hippodrome. From this point on, La Castellana loses its character as a boulevard to become a main route for fast-moving traffic.

Two views of ''La Castellana''. Below, left, the entrance to the National Library.

*Paseo de
la Castellana.
(Below)
Plaza de
San Juan
de la Cruz.*

View of Calle de Alcalá, the Puerta de Alcalá and, left, the Parque del Retiro.

Calle de Alcalá

Madrid's most famous street and one of its longest. A visit, however, is only really worthwhile to the stretch between Puerta del Sol and Plaza de la Independencia.

The origins of this street date back to the successive absorption into the city of stretches of the road to the university city of Alcalá de Henares. It is, therefore, a route which has always born much traffic and which has been transformed over the years. Gone are the *huertas*, the olive fields, inns and carriage stations, replaced in the epoque of the Austrias by hospitals, Calvaries, convents and churches, of which only the Church of Las Calatravas has sur-

vived, though the convent of this military order was demolished in 1872.

A little further on, where this street meets the Gran Vía, we find another church whose convent was demolished and which is now the Parish Church of San José. Built in 1733 by Pedro de Ribera on the site of an earlier church, its front contains features typical of this artist, with brickwork framed by chains of stone and, above all, the notable vertical axis which, beginning at the porch, rises up to the very top of the building.

In the second half of the 18th century, Calle Alcalá changed its religious character to become a centre of finance, one of the first constructions illustrative

Front of the Church of the Calatravas (18th century).

of this transformation being the Real Casa de la Aduana. However, it was not until the 20th century that the street took on its present aspect, when it was chosen as the site for the headquarters of banks, insurance companies and large companies in development which made this one of the most elegant districts in Madrid and in which space was also left for the arts, culture and diversion, as is demonstrated by the buildings of the Royal Academy of Fine Arts of San Fernando, the Fine Arts Circle and the Casino of Madrid. At the end of this stretch is the Puerta de Alcalá.

A view of Calle Alcalá.

Gran Via, adjoining Calle Alcalá.

The Gran Vía

A street well worth a visit, lively and full of shops, which achieved fame when only at the project stage through the zarzuela opera ''La Gran Vía''. Work began in 1910 following the plans of López Salaberry and Octavio Palacios.

The stretch between Alcalá and the Red de San Luis is the most homogenous, containing buildings dating back to 1914-17, uniformly characterised by an eclectic style.

In the second stretch, between the Red de San Luis and the Plaza del Callao, a boulevard was to have been built, though this idea was finally discarded.

Here, functionality becomes the key architectural characteristic. The most interesting building is one designed by Ignacio Cárdenas in cooperation with the American architect Weeks for the Telefónica company. Madrid's first skyscraper, it was terminated in 1929, permission to construct this 81-metre high building only being granted due its being declared of public utility.

The final stretch begins at the popular Plaza del Callao, one of the busiest squares in the city, flanked on all sides by cinemas and department stores. From this point up to the Plaza de España, the buildings are much more varied in style and height,

A view of Calle Alcalá, showing its junction with Gran Via.

having little in common one with another. Outstanding is the modernity of two of its most characteristic buildings, the Press Palace, designed by Pedro Muguruza in 1924 and the Carrión Building, better-known as Capitol, commenced in 1931 to a project by Luis Martínez Feduchi and Vicente Eced.
Nowadays, the special flavour of this street is provided by the shops, cafés and cinemas which line it, making it one of the busiest and most cosmopolitan areas of Madrid.

The Telefónica Building in Gran Via, the first skyscraper to be built in Madrid.

*Plaza de
Callao and
Gran Via.*

The Chapel of San Isidro was built to house the relics of the body of Saint Isidoro, though these were transferred to the Church of San Isidro in the 18th century.

The Morería district

This is one of the oldest *barrios* of Madrid, whose labyrinth of tiny, irregular-shaped squares and winding streets allow the visitor a glimpse of the layout of the medieval city. To walk the little streets of this district, with their evocative names — Granado, Redondilla, Mancebos, Alfonso VI, or the Alamillo, Morería or Paja squares — so full of history and legend, is to return to a Madrid recently reconquered, in which the Moorish population was confined within this area and from which period the district takes its name. It is certain that this district contained a mosque, probably situated on the site where, in 1312, Alphonse XI ordered the building of the Mudéjar Church of San Pedro el Viejo, of which only the tower has survived.

In the late-15th century, the district began to flourish once more and the palaces of the noble Lasso de Castilla, Vargas, Alvarez de Toledo and Lujanes families were constructed, only to be replaced during the 19th century by the dwelling places which we can contemplate today.

Between the squares of La Paja and Los Carros is one of the most interesting architectural areas of the city, formed by the Church of San Antonio (totally reformed after 1936), the 16th-century Chapel of the Bishop (altarpiece and three tombs, jewels of Castilian Renaissance sculpture) and the Chapel of San Isidro, built in the mid-17th century to house the relics of the patron saint of the city.

Plaza de la Paja ("Straw Square") thus named because straw from the fields belonging to the Bishop's Chapel Foundation was sold here. In the background, the Chapel of the Obispo and the dome of the Chapel of San Isidro.

The Arco de la Victoria in Plaza de la Moncloa, constructed in 1955.

Moncloa and the University City

This area was totally transformed during the years after 1939, with the construction of the General Headquarters of the Air Force, a work in which Luis Gutiérrez Soto attempted to recreate the Herreran and Baroque styles which had characterised earlier architectural periods.

The district is much frequented by young people, as it is in close proximity to the University City, whose entrance can be considered the triumphal arch, con-

The Arco de la Victoria and the buildings of Air Force Headquarters.

"El Relevo de la Antorcha", a work by Ana Vaughn Hyatt located in Ciudad Universitaria.

structed according to a project by Modesto López Otero who, in 1929, commissioned by Alphonse XIII, had already begun to design the buildings and facilities of this university complex. With as its central axis the Avenida Complutense, this area contains the various faculties, sports grounds and colleges of the university, the whole surrounded by pleasant gardens.

Nearby stands the Palace of the Moncloa, official residence of the President of the Government.

The Moncloa Palace.

The lake and extensive gardens of the Casa del Campo, one of the most pleasant and relaxing spots in Madrid.

A view of the Fun Fair in the gardens of the Casa del Campo.

PARKS AND GARDENS

One of the pavilions in the Parque del Retiro.

The Casa del Campo

This is Madrid's largest park, 1,747 hectares of natural landscaping populated by typical Mediterranean vegetation. Its origins go back to the reign of Philip II, who acquired these lands to use as the royal hunting grounds, its ownership passing to the City Council in 1931 by decision of the Second Republic. The park now contains a variety of facilities, such as the Zoo, the Funfair and exhibition area with Crystal Palace and pavilions in which trade fairs are held, as well as numerous snack bars situated around the lake with its rowing boats and other craft.

The Palacio de Cristal, in the Parque del Retiro.

The Retiro Park

This is Madrid's most important park, not because of size (12 hectares) but due to its rich history, as it originally formed part of the Palace of Buen Retiro, constructed in the 17th century by the Count-Duke of Olivares for Philip IV. For this, the Count-Duke employed Italian artists, who conceived the park as a succession of spaces in which plants and trees alternated with ponds, statues or small shrines, forming a veritable labyrinth. This Italian Baroque style was altered in the 18th century with the ascendance to the throne of the Bourbons, from which time on the predominant style employed was of French influence, an example of which is "El Parterre".

The gardens were destroyed during the War of Spanish Succession and began to be reconstructed during the reigns of Ferdinand VII and Isabel II. After the Revolution of September 1868, the nature of the park changed radically, as it became the property of the City Council, and it is now an area where a wide range of leisure activities are available, from sailing and rowing in the lake on whose banks stands the monument to Alphonse XII, many types of sports, exhibitions at the Palace of Velázquez and in the

The lake of the Parque del Retiro, presided over by the statue of Alfonso XII.

Rose garden in the Parque del Retiro.

Monument to the Alvarez Quintero brothers, in the Parque del Retiro.

Crystal Palace or, simply, as the site of pleasant, relaxing walks. Throughout the park are distributed statues dedicated to illustrious Spaniards, such as General Martínez Campos by Benlliure, one of the finest in Madrid.

The Botanical Gardens

Founded in 1781 by Charles III, inspired by the ideas of the Enlightenment, these gardens form part of a cultural centre surrounding the Prado. Built by Juan de Villanueva in the Neo-Classical style popular at the time, the gardens consist of three terraces in which the plantations are organised into geometric figures, circles and squares, on the topmost of which was built the Villanueva Pavilion, used as greenhouse and library.

This upper terrace was reorganised in the mid-19th century, its rationalism giving way to a romantic garden with the creation of a more natural landscape. The other two terraces have been retained in their original form. In the first, known as the Terrace of the Squares, are plants which are useful to humanity, and on the second, known as the Terrace of the Schools, the plants are placed in order, from the most simple to the most highly-developed.

Palacio Villanueva, in the Botanical Gardens.

Temple of Debod in the Cuartel de la Montaña park.

Other parks

There are some forty parks contained in Madrid, with a variety of landscapes: there are romantic and wild areas, open fields, woods and *parterres*. Outstanding are: Campo del Moro, until 1978 the private garden of the Palacio Real, now open to the public, constructed during the reign of Isabel II; the Sabatini Gardens, dating back to the Second Republic and designed by Mercadel, which occupy the site of the Royal Riding Stables, next to the Palacio Real; the West Park (Parque del Oeste), containing, in the area known as the Mountain of the Pious Prince, the Temple of Debod, a gift from the Egyptian government as a mark of gratitude for the cooperation of Spain in the archaeological work at Nubia; and the Park of El Capricho, in the Alameda de Osuna.

Main front of the Prado Museum and the monument to Velázquez.

MUSEUM AND ART COLLECTIONS

Prado Museum (Paseo del Prado)

This beautiful Neo-Classic building by Juan de Villanueva, dating back to 1785, contains the renowned art collection created in 1819 by Ferdinand VII on the initiative of his wife, Isabel of Branganza, donating 311 works from the royal collection of paintings. Later, this fund of works was increased through successive donations on the part of monarchs, pictures from "disentailed" convents, and private donations. The museum now possesses more than 6,000 works, many of which are held in the vaults of the Prado, whilst others have been loaned to different institutions.

The museum takes its name from the avenue on which it stands, the Prado de San Jerónimo, another fruit of the Enlightenment whose construction was inspired by Charles III. Originally, the building was intended to house the Natural Science Museum, but the eruption of the War of Independence altered its destiny. Its groundplan contains three classical architectural elements: the rotunda of the foyer, the temple and the palace, which are communicated by galleries. The structure is simple and decoration rests on the quality of the materials employed, in accordance with the canons of Neo-Classical architecture. The outstanding element is the central portico with six huge Doric columns, reminiscent of Greek temples.

The Descent from the Cross by Van der Weyden.

The Haywain, a triptych considered to have been painted during the early phase of Hieronymus Bosch's artistic development.

"La Maja Desnuda" one of the most famous paintings by Goya, in the Prado.

"Las Meninas", a masterpiece by Velázquez, in the Prado.

Besides its 6,000 paintings, the museum also contains more than 400 classical sculptures and a great many fine treasures, such as the Treasure of the Delfín. There are excellent collections of the works of three of the greatest geniuses in the history of painting, El Greco, Velázquez and Goya, as well as the most splendid anthology of the history of Spanish paintings from its Romanesque origins up to the 19th century. The Prado also contains a wealth of works from the most important European schools, Flemish, Italian, Dutch, French and German, as well the most complete collections in Europe of the works of certain foreign artists, such as Titian, or schools, such as 16th-century Venetian painting. Amongst its many masterpieces, we can mention the following here: "Gentleman with his hand on his chest" and "The Baptism of Christ" by El Greco; "Las Meninas", "The Surrender of Breda", "The Topers", "Philip IV on horseback", "The Count-Duke of Olivares on horseback" and "Christ Crucified" by Velázquez; "La Maja Desnuda", "Charles IV and his family", "The Fusillade of the 3 May" and the *Pinturas Negras*, "Black Paintings", by Goya; "The Emperor Charles V on horseback" by Titian; "Portrait of a Cardinal" and "The Virgin of the Rose" by Raphael; "Man with a golden chain" by Tintoretto; "Jesus and the Centurion" by Veronese; "David and Goliath" by Caravaggio; "Death of the Virgin" by

Mantegna; "Artemis" by Rembrandt; works by Dürer and practically all the finest works of Rubens, Bosch and Breughel.

Besides the previously-mentioned Villanueva Building, the Prado Museum also occupies two other. The first of these is the *Casón del Buen Retiro* (Calle de Alfonso XII, 28) which, with the present-day Army Museum, forms the only surviving remains of the formerly extensive dependences of the Palacio del Buen Retiro. The rooms contain collections of 19th-century Spanish painting, as well as a number of outstanding contemporary works. The second is the Palacio de Villahermosa.

Thyssen Bornemisza Collection Foundation
(Paseo del Prado, 8)

Housed in the Palacio de Vistahermosa, this comprises an important, if temporary, collection of works spanning from the early Italian painters to the pop at era (13th to 20th century).

"Gentleman with his hand on his chest", a portrait by El Greco, in the Prado.

The Casón del Buen Retiro, annex to the Prado Museum.

National Archaeological Museum (Calle Serrano, 13) Founded in 1867 by Isabel II with funds from various institutions, this had as its first home, until 1895, the Casino de la Reina (at the end of Calle de Embajadores), after which it was transferred to its present site, at the back of the building housing the National Library.

After many difficulties, the museum was totally reorganised in a transformation which tripled its exhibition space and made profound alterations to its criteria regarding exhibitions, giving it a pronouncedly didactic orientation and making it a model to be imitated.

The museum's more than forty rooms offer a complete panoramic view of the ancient cultures of the Earth. Besides its excellent reproductions of the cave paintings of Altamira, it also contains such treasures as the three *damas* of Iberian sculpture, from Elche, Baza and Cerro de los Santos, the collection of votive crowns from Guarrazar, a splendid collection of coins, a remarkable display of precious stones and porcelain from the Palace of the Buen Retiro, pottery, Greek and Etruscan urns, Greek and Roman sarcophagi and mausoleums and many other artistic pieces of outstanding interest.

The entrance to the National Archaeological Museum.

The votive crown of Recesvinto, from Guarrazar, one of the fine examples of Visigothic art in the Archaeological Museum.

The Reina Sofia Art Centre stages exhibitions of contemporary art. In the photograph, Picasso's ''Guernica''.

Reina Sofia Art Centre (Calle Santa Isabel, 52)
This centre occupies the huge building of the former Hospital of San Carlos, designed by the architect Sabatini, commissioned by Charles III. It is now dedicated to contemporary art in all its manifestations, with permanent and temporary exhibitions of Spanish and international art and artists. Its reference library is one of the most important in Europe.

A view of the Reina Sofia Art Centre.

OTHER MUSEUMS

The museums mentioned above are the most important in Madrid and their priceless collections make a visit to them highly recommended to any visitor. However, there are many more museums in the city, which also make interesting visits. Some of these are: the Royal Academy of Fine Arts (Calle de Alcalá, 13), with an important collection of painting and sculpture; the Municipal Museum (Calle de Fuencarral, 78), containing paintings and other objects relating to the history of Madrid; the National Ethnological Museum (Calle de Alfonso XII, 68), with exhibits illustrating the primitive cultures of the five continents; the Lázaro Galdiano Museum (Calle de Serrano, 12), an important private art collection; the Romantic Museum (Calle de San Mateo, 13), an interesting reproduction of a palace from that period; the Decorative Arts Museum (Calle de Montalbán, 12); the Army Museum (Calle de Méndez Núñez, 1); the Royal Tapestry Factory (Calle de Fuenterrabia, 2); the Natural Science Museum (Calle de José Abascal, 2); and the Wax Museum (Paseo de Recoletas, 41), etc.

Two rooms in the Cerralbo Museum, a palace housing the various collections of the Marquis of Cerralbo, converted into a museum on his death in 1924, in accordance with the conditions of his will.

The Army Museum houses a fine collection of armour,
among it that of the Gran Capitán.

View of the Fiesta *of the ''Modistillas''.*

Couples dancing the popular ''chotis''.

POPULAR FESTIVITIES AND BULLFIGHTS

The inhabitants of Madrid have always been great lovers of street festivities to celebrate important dates. On 5 January is the Procession of the Magi, which follows a route through all the main streets of the city, and in February, Carnival officially commences with the inaugural address of the Muse of this *fiesta*, who also presides over the procession along La Castellana and Recoletos, with prizes for the best floats. During this festivity, there are joke-telling competitions and dances organised by the City Council, and Carnival ends on Ash Wednesday with the Burial of the Sardine, which is accompanied by a mournful procession.

At Easter, many processions take place, outstanding of which are: those of the Poor Jesus, the Great Power and the *Macarena* on the Thursday; those of Jesus of Medinaceli, the *Dolorosa* and the Silence on Good Friday, when the Christ Procession also takes place in the cloisters of the Convent of the Descalzas, led by a magnificent wooden statue by Gaspar Becerra; and, lastly, on Easter Saturday, the Holy Burial, which takes place in Plaza Mayor.

On 2 May is the commemoration of the Autonomous Community of Madrid, with the organisation of numerous cultural and leisure activities, but the most important festivities take place on May 15, day of Saint Isidro, patron saint of the city, with concerts, theatre performances, puppet shows and passacaglias, book and craft fairs, dances lasting well into the early hours and firework displays. All this in stark contrast with the day of the other patron saint of the city, that of the Virgin of the Almudena (November 9), which passes by practically unnoticed.

At the beginning of December, the city begins to prepare for the Christmas festivities, after which the population sees the old year out on 31 December to

"El Barquillo", typically Madrilenian.

Las Ventas Bullring is the largest in Spain.

the chimes of the clock in the Puerta del Sol. The New Year is welcomed with particular enthusiasm by the crowd gathered in this square.

Throughout the year, *fiestas* are celebrated in the various *barrios* or districts of Madrid, of which the most outstanding and traditional are: that of Saint Anthony of La Florida, on 13 June; those of the Virgin of Carmen, on 16 July; and those of Saint Cayetano, Saint Lawrence and La Paloma in the first half of August.

Since medieval times, the most popular entertainment in Madrid has been bullfighting. In the 17th century, every opportunity was taken to hold bullfights in the Plaza Mayor and in 1754 King Ferdinand VI commissioned the architects Ventura Rodríguez and Francisco Moradillo to build a bullring to hold twelve thousand spectators. By the early-20th century, this ring was found to be too small to hold all those wishing to attend the *fiesta nacional* and the bullring of the Plaza Monumental de las Ventas was constructed by José Espelius and Manuel Muñoz Monasterio, who designed it in the Mudéjar style characteristic of many bullrings, with brick walls and ceramic decoration. With a capacity of 22,000, it is the largest in Spain and is also considered the most important, the top bullfighters appearing here as if taking an exam before a demanding and knowledgeable crowd. Between 70 and 72 bullfights are held at "Las Ventas" every year, the season beginning in April, but the high point is during the Saint Isidro Fair, when the ring holds capacity audiences for a total of 26 bullfights, three of which are usually with young bulls and another two on horseback. After the Fair, bullfights continue to be held every Sunday and on some important holidays, the most important events being the Charity and Press *corridas*. The season ends with the four or five bullfights of the Autumn Fair.

The visitor to Madrid will find here all manner of nightspots, from traditional bars and restaurants to open-air terraces.

The Arco de Cuchilleros, a nook which forms part of "Old Madrid".

THE NIGHTLIFE OF MADRID

There can be no city which offers the quantity and variety of night-spots as Madrid, a city where diversion is available at any hour of the day or night. Outstanding are the cafés, heirs of those which hosted the famous gatherings of the 19th and early-20th centuries. Much, even now, have preserved their original decor and atmosphere, with private salons, whilst others have been brought more up to date and offer music, exhibitions, games, etc. When we speak of going out at night in Madrid, however, we have to speak in terms of ''zones'' in which all types of night-spots are to be found, from restaurants where we can eat to our heart's content to bars and discotheques offering a vast variety of music, live and on record, in settings to suit all tastes. These ''zones'' include Huertas, Alsonso Martínez, Malasaña, Lavapiés, Orense, Moncloa, Cea Bermúdez, the terraces of Paseo de la Castellana and ''Old Madrid''.

Lovers of dancing will find in Madrid a whole spectrum of styles, from discotheques for the young, in which alcohol and smoking are not allowed, to the classical dance hall with band and music from the 1940s to the 1960s. Without forgetting, of course, the typical Flamenco *tablaos*, where we can enjoy the show or even take part in it, and the clubs, offering comedy and variety shows.

Two typical spots.

EATING OUT: TAVERNS AND RESTAURANTS

There are a number of fine dishes which, although they originated in other areas, have become typical of Madrid and can now be considered local. *Cocido*, stew, is the most typical dish of the city, followed by *gallinejas*, fried pieces of chicken, *entresijos*, similar to tripe, snails, garlic soups (unlike in other parts of Spain, cooked without egg) and, turning to sweets, *churros* and *porras*, dough deep-fried in batter, San Isidro doughnuts and the new sweets which have become popular at local festivities, such as the ''Crown of the Almudena'' or the ''Community Tart'', created by the Pastry-makers Association. The finest local drinks include wines from San Martín de Valdeiglesias, Colmenar de Oreja and Arganda and the distinctive liquer made from madrona.

Besides the typical dishes, Madrid also offers specialities from all the regions of Spain and from other countries, and, according to one's pocket, it is possible to choose between five-star restaurants and the cheapest businessman's lunch. Or, more informally, to eat ''tapas'' at any of the infinity of taverns, beer-houses and bars to be found all over the city.

Mention should be made of those eating-houses which have dedicated more than 100 years to the service of the palates of the people of Madrid, such as Lhardy, Antonio Sánchez or Botín, and whose salons have witnessed whole chapters of the history of Madrid.

Typical Madrilenian dishes: cocido, callos (tripe) and chocolate con churros.

Madrid contains both traditional emporia and modern shopping galleries.

area with the young, and the AZCA and Calle Orense district. In most of these zones there are also department stores for greater convenience.

There are also many streets in Madrid which have become specialised in some particular product or service, such as Calle del Prado, where there are a great number of antique shops, Calle del Barquillo, where music and video equipment is the speciality, Calle de Libreros and surrounding area, where books of all kinds, from the oldest to the most recent publications can be found, and Calle del Almirante, centre of the most up-to-date fashions.

Alongside the traditional shops, some with more than 100 years' existence, have grown up huge shopping centres, supermarkets, department stores, bars, restaurants, banks, cinemas, discotheques and other leisure centres.

Madrid is also the site of various open-air markets, chiefly open on Sundays and holiday mornings. These include the stamp and coin market of the Plaza Mayor, the book fair open daily in the Cuesta de Moyano and the flea markets of Ventas and Tetuán. The Rastro is the most famous of these flea markets and also the most interesting. It is situated between Plaza de Cascorro and Ronda de Toledo, taking Calle Ribera de Curtidores as its central axis. Its origins go back to the 16th century, when the area contained the slaughterhouse, known as the ''rastro'', around which other traders established their businesses. These were followed in the 19th century by the second-hand clothes and junk dealers, who in turn gave way to antique shops and auction houses. However, the Rastro of the present day is chiefly characterised by the infinity of street dealers selling absolutely everything and the crowds of people who, looking out for a bargain, or simply enjoying the colourful scene, fill these streets with bustling life.

MARKETS, BOUTIQUES AND SHOPPING CENTRES

Shopping in Madrid presents no difficulties, for there are a number of areas in which shops are concentrated in such a way as to make the job an easy one. According to budget, the visitor can choose between the exclusive luxury boutiques of the Salamanca district, the centre, along the Gran Vía and around the Puerta del Sol, Princesa and Moncloa, a popular

Various views of the
"Rastro" flea market,
and a stand in the
stamp and coin market
in Plaza Mayor.

The Madrid Planetarium was opened in 1984.

LEISURE AND CULTURAL ACTIVITIES

Throughout the year, Madrid offers a wide range of cultural activies, some on a permanent basis, such as its cinemas, theatres, exhibition halls and cultural centres, others temporary, including the fairs, festivals and seasons which take place annually.

Regarding films, the choice is unbeatable, with more thann 100 salons showing from the latest Spanish or international productions to old favourites and classics projected in original version with subtitles in Spanish. The labour of the *Filmoteca* is invaluable in this field, showing as it does films of all types and periods, nationalities, styles and directors.

The 35 theatres of Madrid, at which both private and national companies perform, offer the complete panorama of dramatic art, including the review, verse drama and puppet shows.

Lovers of all kinds of music will also find satisfaction in Madrid, where the widest possible variety of performances are continually offered: chamber concerts, large orchestras, zarzuela, jazz and modern music in all its manifestations are ever-present on the music programmes.

Madrid's Teatro Real is a centre permanently devoted to opera.

Cultural life in the city is also promoted through the activities of an infinity of institutions and art galleries and, finally, we should mention the leisure activities offered by the Casa del Campo Zoo, the Planetarium, the Aquarium and the Fun Fair.

The Santiago Bernabeu Football Stadium, built in 1946, was modernised for the 1982 World Cup.

SPORT

The sports facilities of Madrid are such that it is possible to view as a spectator, or take part in as a player, a huge number of different sports. Swimming pools, sports complexes, open-air courts and circuits, the *Palacio de los Deportes*, the Zarzuela Race-track and the Dog-track and, of course, the great football stadiums, the Santiago Bernabeu and the Vicente Calderón are but a few of the facilities on offer. Mountaineers and lovers of water sports are catered for at the nearby mountains and lakes and reservoirs, and exciting car and motor bike races are held at the Jarama Circuit.

The Vicente Calderón Football Stadium.

Main front of the Palacio de El Pardo.

ENVIRONS OF MADRID

Palace of El Pardo

This palace is situated just fourteen kilometres from the centre of the city, surrounded by oak woods and the scrublands of the Mountain of El Pardo, formerly the royal hunting grounds, in which there are rabbits, deer and the occasional wild boar.

El Pardo was constructed under Charles V on the site where, since the 14th century, had stood a royal residence. Destroyed by fire in 1604, Philip III ordered it quickly rebuilt, and the palace was extended over successive reigns, Ferdinand VI enclosing the entire perimeter of the mountain. The Puerta de Hierro and the San Fernando Bridge were constructed during his reign as the entrance to the Royal Residence.

In 1772, Charles III commissioned Francisco Sabatini to build new extensions which gave the palace its present aspect. Charles also ordered the decoration of his rooms with paintings, tapestries, furniture, lamps and clocks which are still preserved here. After the Civil War, it became the residence of General Franco, and after his death the palace was converted into a museum and the temporary residence of visiting heads of state. Nearby is the *cottage orné* of the *Casita del Príncipe*, the Palace of La Quinta and the Church of the Capuchins Monastery, housing a Christ by Gregorio Fernández, considered a masterpiece of Spanish 17th-century religious sculpture.

Palace of the Zarzuela

Now the official residence of the King and Queen of Spain, this was constructed in the 17th century according to plans drawn up by Juan Gómez de Mora and Alonso Carbonell. Completely destroyed during the Civil War, it was rebuilt in 1960 as a faithful reproduction of the original.

Aranjuez

This beautiful city stands just 46 kilometres from Madrid, and is a splendid example of Baroque town planning, converted into a royal residence by Philip V and the scene of many of the most important events in the history of Spain. The *Palacio Real* is an impressive building surrounded by magnificent gardens and containing rich decoration, furniture, tapestries, painting and a magnificent Porcelain Room whose walls and ceiling are covered with porcelain from the Royal Factory of El Buen Retiro. Also worthy of a visit are the houses known as the *Casa del Labrador* and the *Casa de Marinos*.

Palacio de la Zarzuela.

The Aranjuez Gardens conserve the Rococo style of the original, replete with statues and fountains.

The Monastery of El Escorial is characterised by its Monumental style.

El Escorial

This immense monastery, built by Philip II, stands at the foot of the Guadarrama Sierra, 49 kilometres from Madrid. Work began in 1563 under the direction of Juan Bautista de Toledo and was completed 21 years later by Juan de Herrera. Besides the monastery and royal pantheon, the site also contains the Palace of the Bourbons, the college, the library and the Courtyard of the Kings, which gives access to the church.

Nearby is the *Casita del Príncipe*, the *Casita de Arribau* and the site known as the "Chair" of Philip II, from where one commands a magnificent view of the monastery.

The Valley of the Fallen

Situated in the Cuelgamuros Valley, this is an impressive basilica ordered built by General Franco, cut out of the cliff face of a rock on which stands a huge cross, 150 metres high, flanked by gigantic statues representing the Apostles and the cardinal virtues.

Chinchón: the church and typical houses seen from Plaza Mayor.

The Alcazar of Toledo and Aqueduct of Segovia.

Other places of interest

Also near to Madrid are Alcalá de Henares, with its university, Church of San Justo and the Bernadine Convent; Chinchón, with 15th-century castle and charming square; the Monastery of El Paular, in the splendid setting of the Lozoya Valley; Manzanares el Real, with a castle built in 1435 by the Marquis of Santillana; and the cities of Toledo, Avila, Segovia and Cuenca, all within easy reach of Madrid and linked to it by good communications.

◁ The Santa Cruz, in the Valley of the Fallen.

Contents

Printed in EEC by FISA - Escudo de Oro, S.A.

ESCUDO DE ORO, S.A. COLLECTIONS

ALL SPAIN

1 MADRID
2 BARCELONA
3 SEVILLE
4 MAJORCA
5 THE COSTA BRAVA
8 CORDOBA
9 GRANADA
10 VALENCIA
11 TOLEDO
12 SANTIAGO
13 IBIZA and Formentera
14 CADIZ and provincia
15 MONTSERRAT
17 TENERIFE
20 BURGOS
24 SEGOVIA
25 SARAGOSSA
26 SALAMANCA
27 AVILA
28 MINORCA
29 SAN SEBASTIAN and Guipúzcoa
30 ASTURIAS
31 LA CORUNNA and the Rías Altas
32 TARRAGONA
40 CUENCA
41 LEON
42 PONTEVEDRA, VIGO and Rías Bajas
43 RONDA
46 SIGUENZA
47 ANDALUSIA
48 CANTABRIA
52 EXTREMADURA
54 MORELLA
58 VALLDEMOSSA

GUIDES

1 MADRID
2 BARCELONA
3 LA RIOJA
4 MAJORCA
6 SANTIAGO DE COMPOSTELA
7 SEVILLA
8 ANDALUCIA
9 GRAN CANARIA
12 GALICIA
13 CORDOBA
14 COSTA BLANCA
15 GRANADA
21 SALAMANCA
22 SEGOVIA
25 AVILA
26 HUESCA
28 TOLEDO
30 SANTANDER

4 LONDON

1 LA HABANA VIEJA
2 EL CAPITOLIO (CUBA)

1 MOROCCO

ALL EUROPE

1 ANDORRA
2 LISBON
3 LONDON
4 BRUGES
6 MONACO
7 VIENNA
11 VERDUN
12 THE TOWER OF LONDON
13 ANTWERP
14 WESTMINSTER ABBEY
15 THE SPANISH RIDING
SCHOOL IN VIENNA
17 WINDSOR CASTLE
18 LA CÔTE D'OPAL
19 COTE D'AZUR
22 BRUSSELS
23 SCHÖNBRUNN PALACE
25 CYPRUS
26 HOFBURG PALACE
27 ALSACE
28 RHODES
30 CORFU
31 MALTA
32 PERPIGNAN
33 STRASBOURG
34 MADEIRA + PORTO SANTO
35 CERDAGNE - CAPCIR
36 BERLIN
42 CONFLENT-CANIGOU

TOURISM

1 COSTA DEL SOL
2 COSTA BRAVA
3 ANDORRA
4 ANTEQUERA
6 MENORCA
8 MALLORCA
9 TENERIFE
14 LA ALPUJARRA
15 LA AXARQUIA
16 PARQUE ARDALES AND EL CHORRO
17 NERJA
18 GAUDI
19 BARCELONA
21 MARBELLA
23 LA MANGA DEL MAR MENOR
25 CATEDRAL DE LEON
26 MONTSERRAT
34 RONDA
35 IBIZA-FORMENTERA
37 GIRONA
38 CADIZ
39 ALMERIA
40 SAGRADA FAMILIA
42 FATIMA
43 LANZAROTE
44 MEZQUITA HASSAN II
45 JEREZ DE LA FRONTERA
46 PALS
47 FUENGIROLA
48 SANTILLANA DEL MAR
49 LA ALHAMBRA Y EL GENERALIFE
50 ABADIA DE WESTMINSTER
51 MONACO-MONTECARLO

ALL AMERICA

1 PUERTO RICO
2 SANTO DOMINGO
3 AREQUIPA
4 COSTA RICA
6 CARACAS
7 LA HABANA
8 LIMA
9 CUZCO

ALL AFRICA

1 MOROCCO
2 THE SOUTH OF MOROCOO
3 TUNISIA

ART IN SPAIN

1 PALAU DE LA MUSICA CATALANA
2 GAUDI
3 PRADO MUSEUM I
(Spanish Painting)
4 PRADO MUSEUM I
(Foreing Painting)
5 MONASTERY OF GUADALUPE
7 THE FINE ARTS MUSUEM OF SEVILLE
10 THE CATHEDRAL OF GIRONA
11 GRAN TEATRO DEL LICEO
(Great Opera House
12 ROMANICO CATALAN
14 PICASSO
15 ROYAL PALACE OF SEVILLE
19 THE ALHAMBRA AND THE GENERALIFE
21 ROYAL ESTATE OF ARANJUEZ
22 ROYAL ESTATE OF EL PARDO
24 ROYAL PALACE OF SAN ILDEFONSO
26 OUR LADY OF THE PILLAR OF
SARAGOSSA
27 TEMPLE DE LA SAGRADA FAMILIA
28 POBLET ABTEI
29 THE CATHEDRAL OF SEVILLE
30 THE CATHEDRAL DE MAJORCA
32 MEZQUITA DE CORDOBA
33 GOYA
34 THE CATHEDRAL OF BARCELONA
35 CASA - MUSEU CASTELL GALA-DALI
PUBOL
36 THE CATHEDRAL OF SIGUENZA
37 SANTA MARIA LA REAL DE NAJERA
38 CASA - MUSEU SALVADOR DALI
PORT LLIGAT

MONOGRAPHS (S)

5 SOLAR ENERGY IN THE CERDAGNE
10 MORELLA
20 CAPILLA REAL DE GRANADA
31 CORDILLERAS DE PUERTO RICO
38 GIBRALTAR
50 BRUGES
68 MONASTERIO DE PIEDRA
70 TORREVIEJA
74 VALLDEMOSSA
75 ANTWERP
84 CATHEDRAL OF MAJORCA
85 CATHEDRAL OF BARCELONA
86 VALL D'UXO

MONOGRAPHS (L)

5 PUERTO RICO
6 THE OLD SAN JUAN
9 THE CITY OF BRUGES
19 MURALLAS DE SAN JUAN

MAPS

1 MADRID
2 BARCELONA
6 LONDON
8 ALICANTE
20 PANAMA
31 SEVILLE
33 BRUGES
36 SEGOVIA
37 CORDOBA
38 CADIZ
40 PALMA OF MAJORCA
45 JEREZ DE LA FRONTERA
47 AVILA
48 ANDORRA
50 SALAMANCA
52 LEON
53 BURGOS
58 IBIZA
78 GRANADA
80 MONACO
93 MENORCA
94 LA MANGA DEL MAR MENOR
96 COSTA BRAVA
97 LLORET DE MAR
98 SANTANDER

Protegemos el bosque; papel procedente de cultivos forestales controlados
Wir schützen den Wald. Papier aus kontrollierten Forsten.
We protect our forests. The paper used comes from controlled forestry plantations
Nous sauvegardons la forêt: papier provenant de cultures forestières contrôlées

Text, photographs, lay-out, design and printing by
EDITORIAL ESCUDO DE ORO, S.A.
Rights of total or partial reproduction and translation reserved.
Copyright of this edition for photographs and text:
© EDITORIAL ESCUDO DE ORO, S.A.
6th Edition - I.S.B.N. 84-378-1551-7
Dep. Legal. B. 1110-1999

MADRID